I0069717

Introduction

Most people procrastinate due to the lack of TIME MANAGEMENT. Especially women. We are overwhelmed by the number of "To Do's" that are on our list which seem to NEVER EVER EVER go away. Some even excel at procrastinating and could win an Olympic medal for their abilities. LOL! If you fall into the category of "an excellent procrastinator," shout "OUCH!" and then say "Bye" to procrastination and "Hello" to TIME MANAGEMENT. Unless you learn how to manage your time, you will never become the best YOU!

Time Killer: Procrastination

"The difference between successful people and very successful people is that very successful people say NO to almost everything." ~ Warren Buffet

Table of Contents

Time Killer: Procrastination

When you research healthcare professionals' idea of why we procrastinate, the first thing that they mention is people put off unpleasant tasks because they are uncomfortable about something. Well, that is half true. The other half is that we also put off things that are not difficult. It is part of the mindset that has developed over the last 50 years. In this microwave society where everything is wanted fast and now, we hear the little voice in our head saying "Hey, you're tired! It can wait until tomorrow. Ain't Married to Medicine on?" Oh...my bad. That's just my voice. The beehive activity that we face on a daily basis leads us to look for any reason to put off not only difficult tasks but items that may even bring us a bit of pleasure...just not enough pleasure to get us to move.

PROCRASTINATE - to put off till another day or time; defer; delay.

Procrastination is a habit that will need to be broken in order to master time management. You will have to "stay woke" hourly, daily and weekly, in order to recognize when procrastination is rearing its ugly head. When you have a task that needs to be completed and you find yourself immediately thinking that going for ice cream might help get you in the mood (...oops! Interjecting my thoughts again. LOL! Sorry.) ...try a simple suggestion.

Tell yourself that you are going to procrastinate right now on that procrastinating thought. That's right, you are going to put off procrastinating and maybe you will procrastinate tomorrow. LOL! Really, give it a try. You will be surprised how that works. But, if that is too farfetched for you, do the following.

SPRINTING - a brief spell of great activity.

Wake up, pick a task and do it for 3-5 minutes. Need to make calls? Then pick up the phone and blast them out. Reward yourself with a hot cup of coffee and do another round of 3-5 minutes. Have a long hot massaging shower and yes, do another 3-5 minutes. The next day build on the day before and go for 5-10 minutes, doing your calls or whatever you picked. Perhaps it was writing and you just keep putting it off. In some Kindle writing groups, they call this method "sprinting." They blast out words for 20 minutes straight, then have a reward and blast away again and they tell each other in the group that they are in the sprint...going as fast as they can. What an accomplishment you will feel when you check your list at the end of the day and you actually accomplished some tasks.

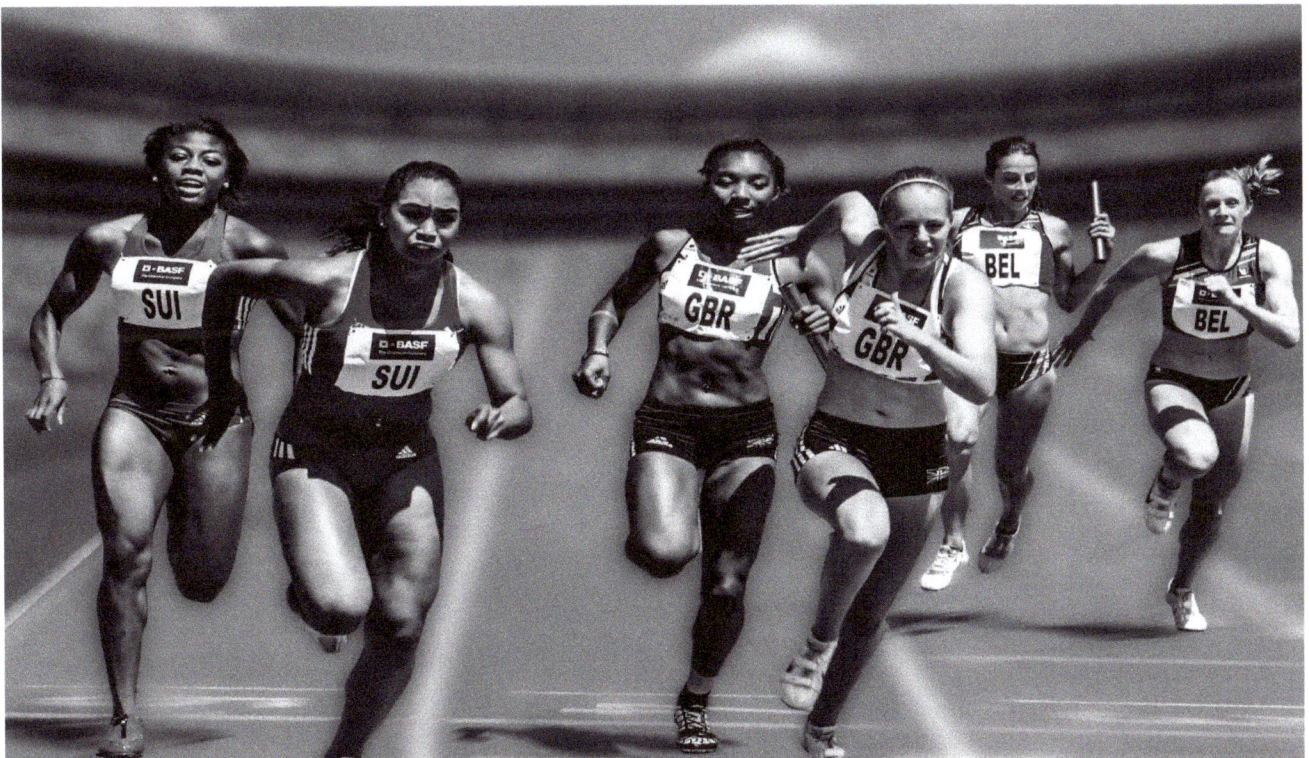

"When your mind controls the matter, what matters most will get done" ~ The REPOSITION Specialist

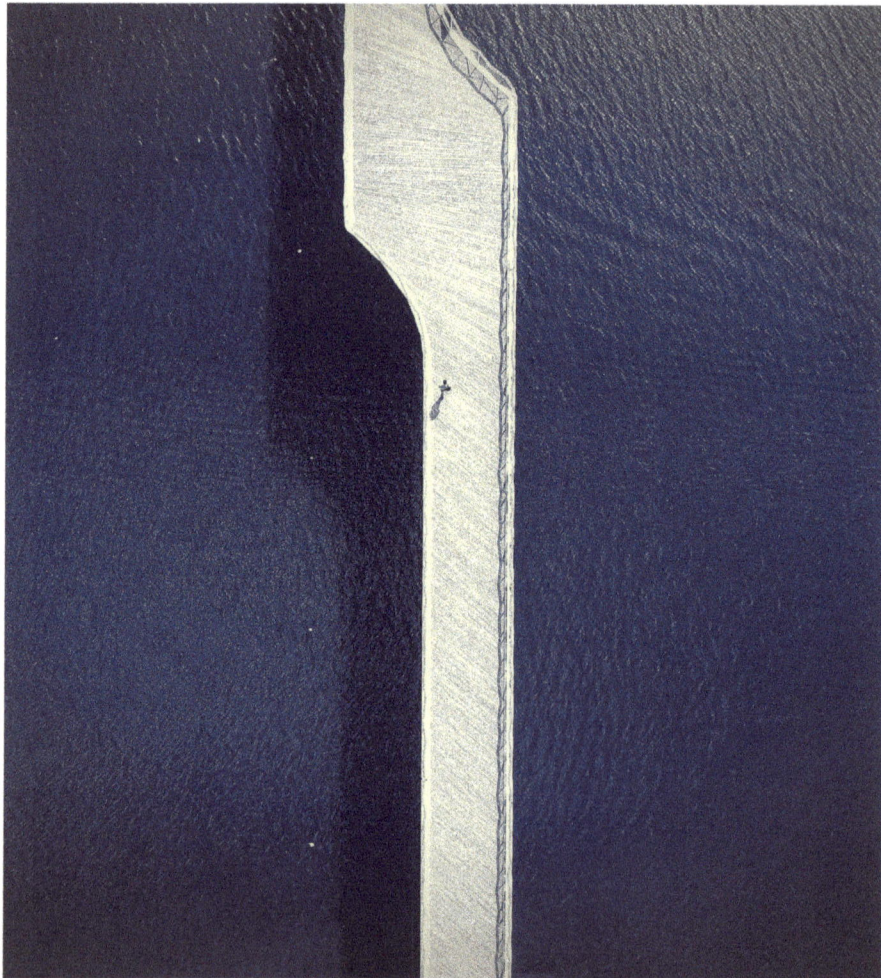

Your mind can take anything and make it seem bigger than it is. Have you heard a noise in your house and then you start thinking about it? You wonder if it's the wind or something about to break down. Suddenly you jump to the idea that it might be a robber or worse, attempting to get into the house. You take a simple noise and blow it up into a full-blown horror movie. Procrastination can be similar in that you think about a task and suddenly it becomes a monster. It will eat you alive, so it is better to turn on Netflix and save the task 'til tomorrow because tomorrow you will slay that dragon.......NOT! Stop blowing tasks up into mythical proportions. One step at a time and GET IT DONE!

SELF-AWARENESS

To become the best YOU, you have to be self-aware of the things that are draining your time. Complete the below activity to uncover what truly is wreaking havoc on your time. Now in order for this exercise to work, you must be brutally honest with yourself. So, get ready, get set..GO!

How do you spend the bulk of your time each day?

_____

_____

_____

_____

_____

_____

_____

_____

_____

_____

_____

_____

_____

_____

_____

_____

_____

_____

_____

_____

_____

_____

_____

_____

_____

_____

_____

_____

Where do you feel that you're not being productive?

How would you rather be spending your time each day?

_____

_____

_____

_____

_____

_____

_____

_____

_____

_____

_____

_____

_____

_____

_____

_____

_____

_____

_____

_____

_____

_____

_____

What are some things you already feel are time wasters?

_____
_____
_____
_____
_____
_____
_____
_____
_____
_____
_____
_____
_____
_____
_____
_____
_____
_____
_____
_____
_____
_____
_____
_____

Focus Focus NOT Hocus Pocus

Focus Focus NOT Hocus Pocus

Gaining and maintaining focus is a major part of productivity. When you have to work long hours, have many things to do, or you have a great deal on your mind, focus goes right out the window. Without the right focus, no matter how many hours you put in or how hard you work, things don't get done well or quickly.

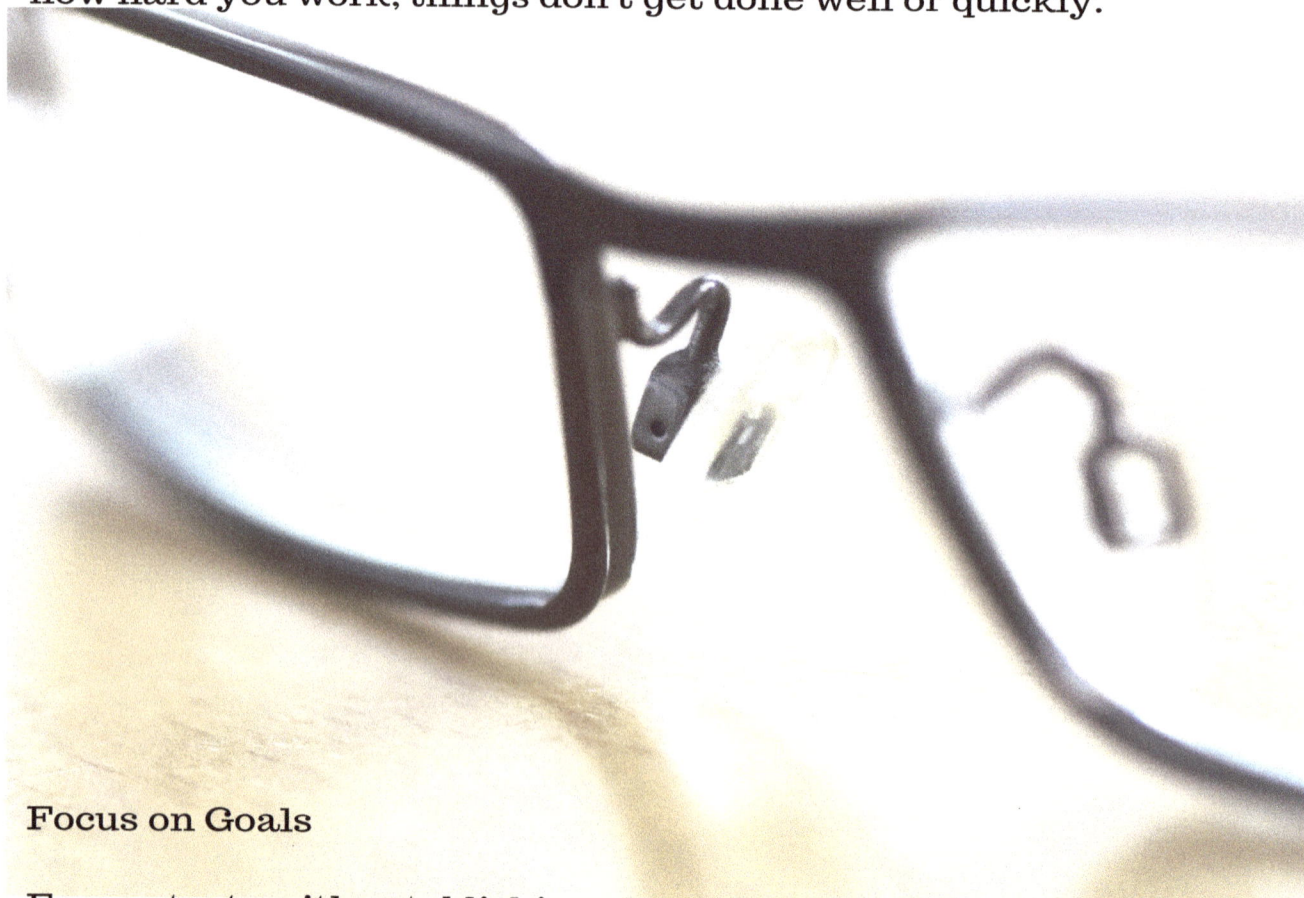

Focus on Goals

Focus starts with establishing clear goals. When you sit down to accomplish a task, that task needs to be at the forefront of your mind. For example, you sit down to write an email to a friend and your focus is stolen away by the Pied Piper of Facebook. If you stay focused on the goal at hand (writing to your friend), you can effectively ignore the lure of social media and get the task done. It's important to stay focused on goals.

To Do or Not To Do

The best way to create focus for the things you have to do each day is to start with goals and from them develop smaller goals (or milestones along the way) and from them, specific tasks.

For example, if you want to clean the house, you have to start with one room and then move on to the next. If you want to create your own internet-based business, you have to start with a business plan, then build a website, and so on. This is how we get things done, by focusing on one task at a time.

Creating a task list is an age-old process. Some may say "It's not that simple. I keep creating them and nothing is getting done." Well there is more to it now than just creating the list. For example, take a large goal and make a list of all of the things that need to be done in order to achieve it. Some items on this list may arrange themselves by priority naturally. Let's say you want to start a business.

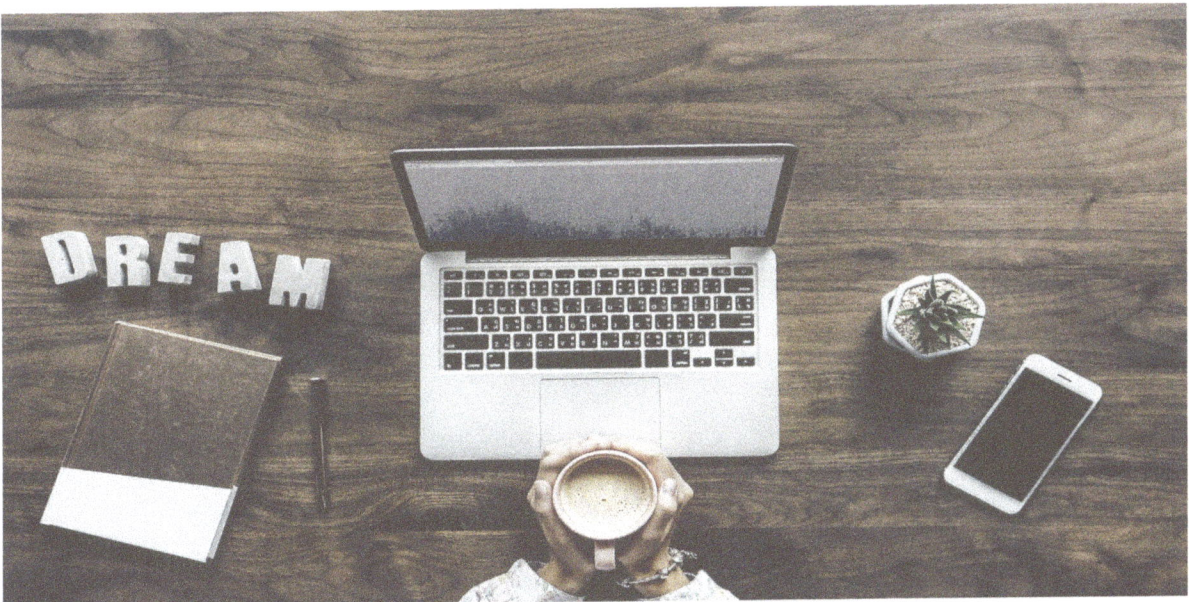

To Do or Not To Do

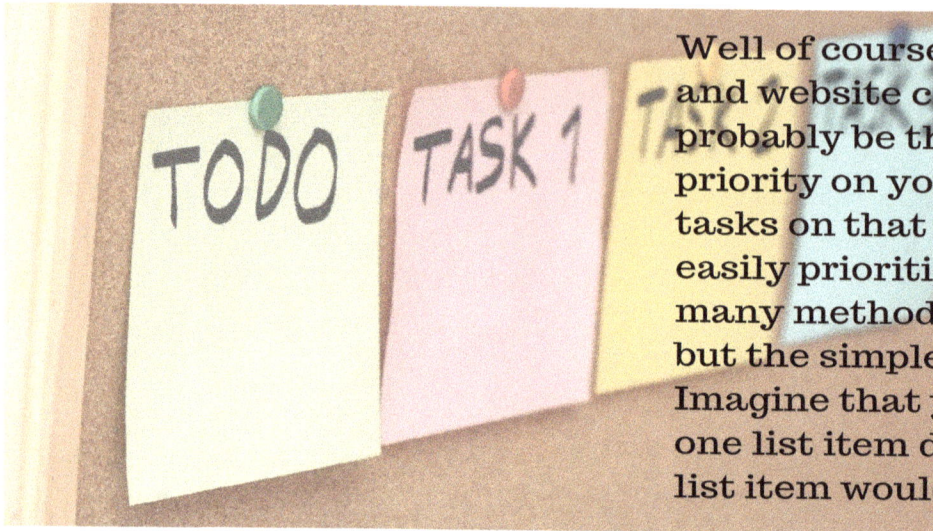

Well of course a business name and website creation would probably be the natural priority on your list. But other tasks on that list aren't so easily prioritized. There are many methods for prioritizing, but the simplest is this: Imagine that you will get only one list item done today. Which list item would it be?

Of course, you'll get more than one item done. But this helps you isolate the first and most important item. Once you've identified this item and put it at the top of your list, repeat. If you could only get two things done today, which of the remaining items would be next? Keep repeating this as you put each list item into its rightful place.

The next step is to assign a deadline to each list item. Not every item on your list may need a real deadline, but by giving each task a deadline, you're putting the list into priority by urgency. Put the item with the closest deadline at the top and organize the rest accordingly.

To Do or Not To Do

There's Only One

After you've listed your tasks and put them in order, you'll have a nicely organized to-do list. You can start at the top and work your way down. This is very simple but there are some ways you can streamline your to-do list for maximum productivity.

First, THERE ONLY SHOULD BE ONE! You should have only one to-do list. If you have many types of things to do today – some work-related, some around the house, some purely for your own enjoyment – you may be tempted to make a different list for each category. But if you do this, you've destroyed the simple beauty of the to-do list. Now you have multiple lists and don't know where to start. Then you are back at procrastination. Nope don't want that to happen.

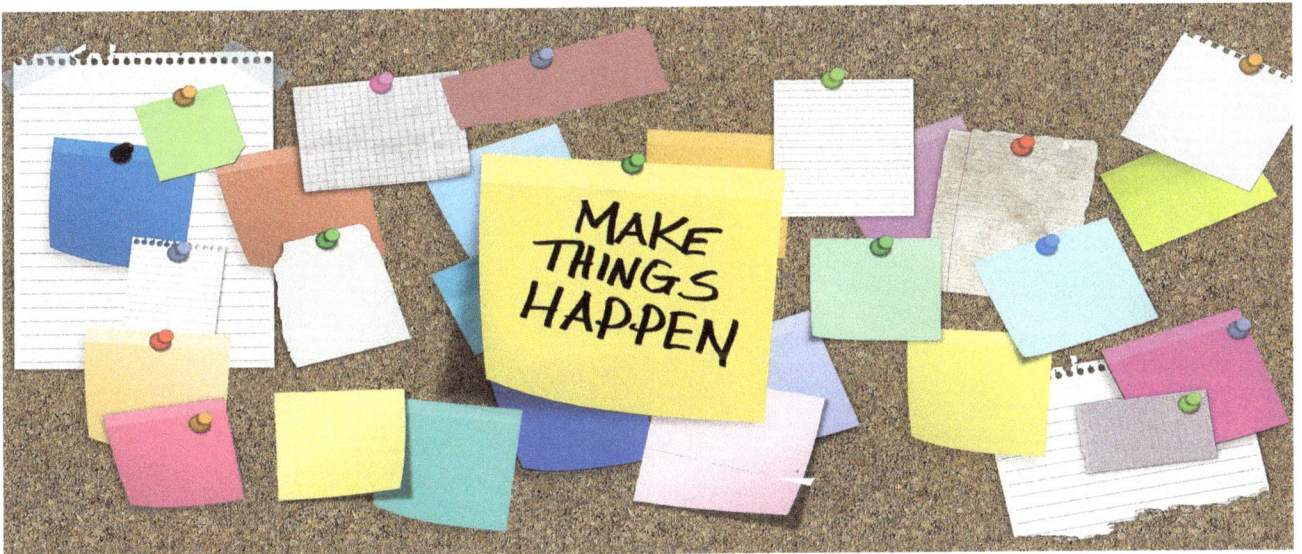

To Do or Not To Do

Instead, you should put everything on one list. You may want to prioritize different item categories or areas. For example, start with work-related tasks. Once those are crossed off your list, tackle the housework or errands. Save the leisure items for the end of the day when you can enjoy them.

Is It Really Necessary?

If you're like many busy people, you love lists. Once you start writing down items into list form, you keep adding everything you can think of until you have a massive list as long as your arm. When this happens, you end up with list clutter, or items you don't really need to have there.

To keep your to-do list under control, it's important to eliminate non-essentials. Think..is it really necessary now? For these non-essential items, create a category on your list titled Non-Essentials. It's good to track these items because if you are like me, if it's not written down, it can surely be forgotten.

To Do or Not To Do

Now please remember that there are only so many hours in a day, so you need to be realistic when setting your daily tasks. If you only have 2 free hours, don't put 50 things on your list. Everything seems to be important and everything appears as if it needs to be done NOW. But if you really take time to think about your tasks and do this exercise, you will see that some things aren't as urgent as you thought.

It's Time To Focus

Time has an important relationship with focus. If you set aside some time to accomplish a task, you can put all of your focus on that task. You know that you have only an hour, so you stay on task. On the other hand, if you work on something for too long, you could start to lose focus and burn out.

A good way to manage time is to take long-term tasks (those that take several hours or days) and break them into bite-sized daily chunks.

To Do or Not To Do

What's the saying..."How do you eat a hamburger? One bite at a time." One suggestion would be to set aside an hour a day for each of your long-term tasks. This allows you enough time to get fully into the task without losing focus. Then, you quit for the day long before you've burned out, and thus you can approach it feeling fresh tomorrow.

One of the best productivity tools in the world is the simple kitchen timer. Setting timers helps you forget about your schedule and just focus on the task. The timer will let you know when it's time to stop. Depending on the nature of the project, you may want to set your timer to go off five minutes before the actual stopping time. This gives you a warning to wrap things up. Of course, with technology at our fingertips, you can use your smartphone, iPad, smart watch or whatever "techy" gadget you may have. The point is...monitor your time to stay on task.

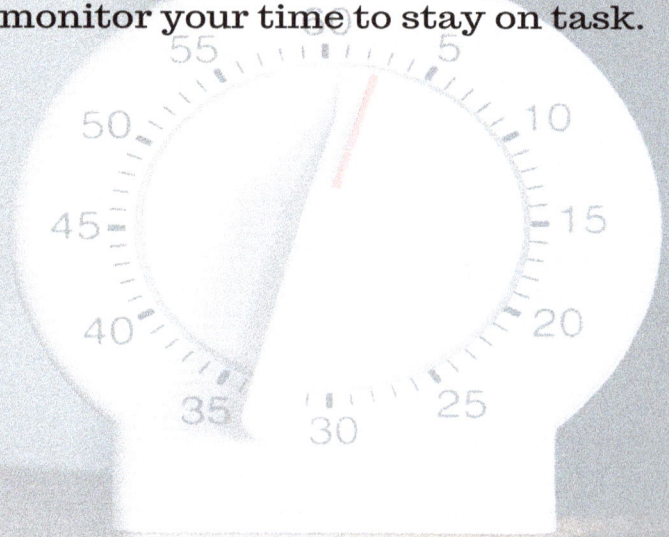

To Do or Not To Do

Multi-Tasking, NOT

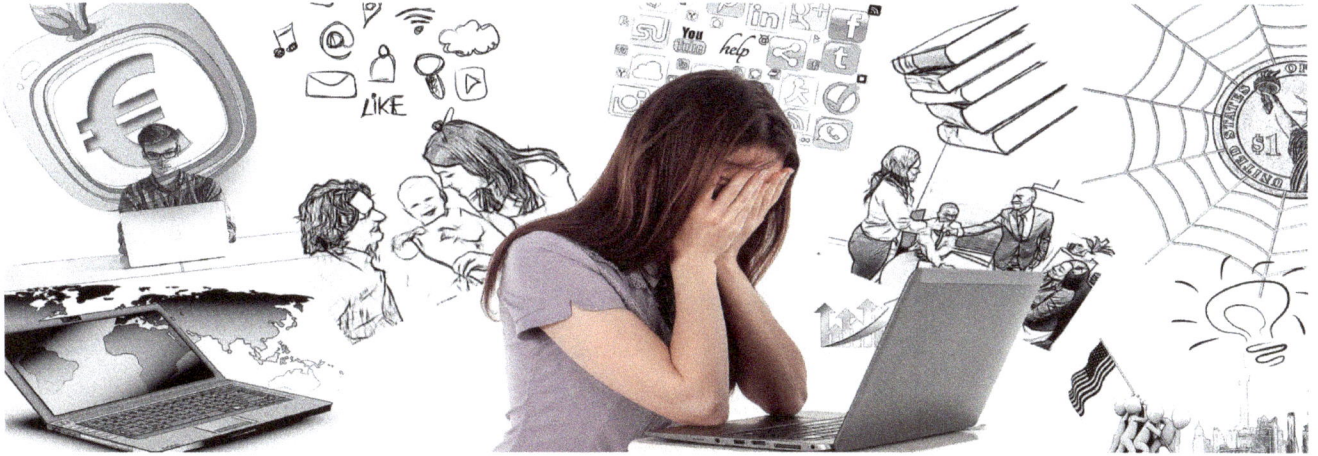

One of the greatest time management myths is the idea that multi-tasking helps you get more done. It makes sense in some ways; by working on several things at once, you're making the best use of your time. But is that really possible? Think about it. Can you really work on more than one thing at the same time? NOPE! You can work on one thing after the other and accomplish them within the same time frame. Example, you can put a pot of water on the stove to start dinner, THEN put a load of clothes in the wash. What you cannot do is put the water on the stove and put the clothes in the wash at the exact same time, which is the definition of multitasking. Unless you are Stretch Armstrong or Mister Fantastic, this is impossible. Trying to "multitask" can ruin your focus. When there are things you can get done within the same time frame, by all means do it but make sure these aren't items that need your undivided attention. Try to work on those items one task at a time.

To Do or Not To Do

Don't Chase the Rabbit

How do you know when you start losing focus? I call it "chasing the rabbit." Maybe it's when you start thinking about other things. Maybe there's a physical response, such as fidgeting or slumping in your chair. Perhaps you have a sudden desire to grab the sides of your head and run from your office screaming, throw your laptop out the window or go for ice cream. LOL!

Learn to recognize the warning signs that tell you you're losing focus. When you feel burnout coming on, set your work aside. Get up from your desk or workstation and physically move to another part of your home or office. Relax and do some other activity to give your brain a break.

To Do or Not To Do

You Killing My Focus...Maaaannn!

I love how Chris Tucker says..."Maaaannn." It's like he's saying, "For real for real." LOL! Seriously though, trying to multitask and burnout are killing your focus. There may be other distractions as well that destroy your focus like TV and one of the biggest culprits, SOCIAL MEDIA. Try to identify these focus killers and develop a strategy for dealing with them. If it's TV, go into a room that doesn't have a TV or put the remote in an inconvenient place when working on a task. You have all kinds of beeps and bell-tones to let you know someone is trying to reach you. These are handy in daily life, but not when you're trying to focus. During the times when you really need to work, turn off all notifications. If necessary, turn your phone off. Yes, OFF, not silent or vibrate, but actually off during the time you are working on a task. If you can't turn it off, let people know that you're busy and unavailable during a certain time or

To Do or Not To Do

give your phone to someone to hold and say, "Only interrupt me if my husband, wife, child or parent calls or if the world blows up... and in that case none of these matter." LOL!

If you have daily focus killers, like if you work at home and your kids get home at three o'clock, no matter how you lock yourself in your office, the sound of the kids getting home might be a distraction. If you can, try to arrange your schedule so that you're taking a break at that time. Give them the focus they need and then get right back to work.

Start Your Day Off Right

We've mostly talked about how to eliminate things that destroy focus which is key to time management, but what about getting into a focused state of mind? The best way to harness your focus is to create a pre-work ritual. These are things you do at the start of your day that gets you into the right state of mind. It could be prayer, meditation, affirmations, yoga, exercise or listening to music. It might be reading a book to get your brain activated. Figure out something that works for you and employ it when you need it.

Improve Your Focus

On the next page, identify and list which things make you lose your focus during the day. For each of these 'focus killers', note which tips from the chapter you're going to implement to improve your focus, and how you'll use them.

Focus Killers Tips to Implement
- Focus on Goals
- Creating a Prioritized To-Do List
- One To-Do List
- Eliminate Non-Essentials
- Scheduling Time for Focus
- No Multi-Tasking
- Know the Warning Signs
- Identify Other Focus Killers
- Develop a Pre-Work Ritual

Improve Your Focus

Focus Killers	Focus Tips

Rhythmless Nation

Rhythmless Nation

Are you a morning person or a night person? Do you have a lull in energy in the afternoon? Do you find that you get more done before lunch than after?

Whether you realize it or not, you have times of the day that are more or less productive. These differ from person to person, but everyone has them. These are your natural energy rhythms and it's important to discover them so that you can use them to your advantage.

Some people wake up early and in the first few hours of the day get more done than most people do the rest of the day. Others spend the day puttering around, seemingly wasting the day away, and then come alive when the sun goes down.

In order to be as productive as possible, you need to work with your natural rhythms. Without realizing it, you may be working against them. For many of us, the regular 9 to 5 schedule is not suitable. By trying to work these regular hours, you may be trying to fit a square peg into a round hole.

What if you have to work 9-5? In that case, you can still use your rhythms to their advantage by identifying the right times of the day for the right kinds of tasks.

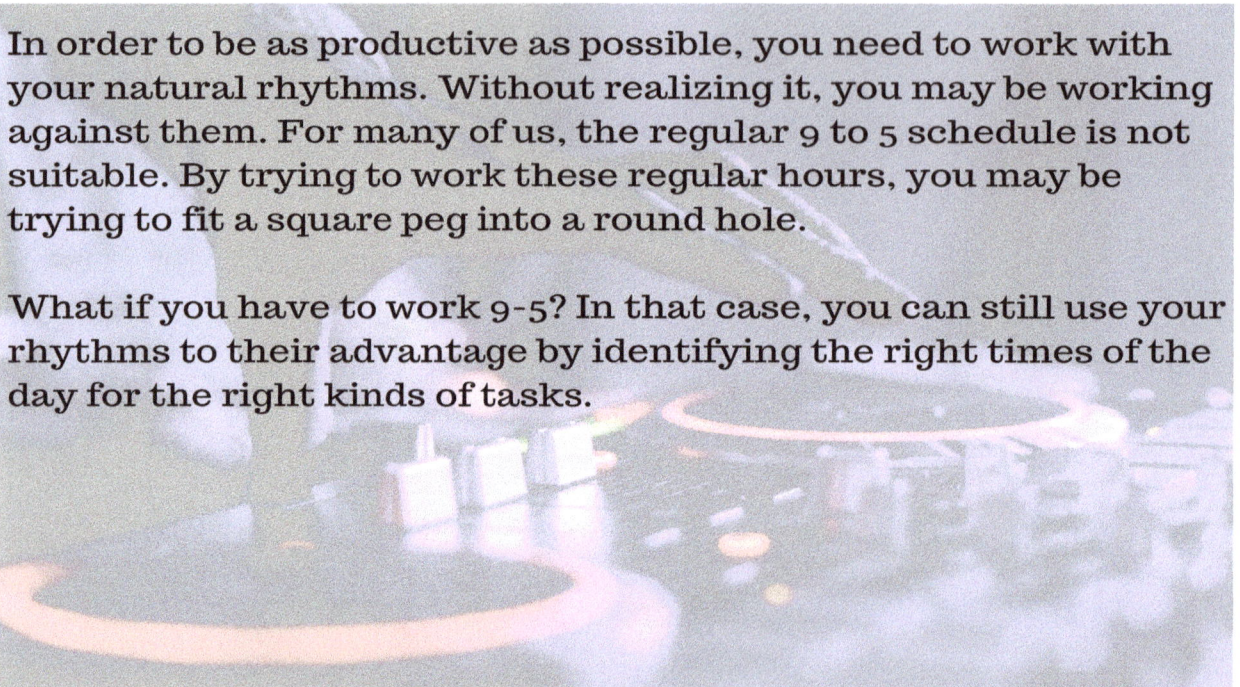

Rhythmless Nation

How to Discover Your Rhythms

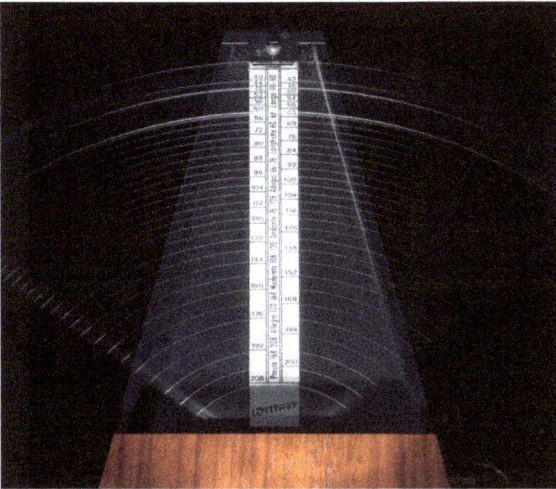

First of all, you may already have some idea of when you work best. If the above questions I asked triggered an immediate answer, you're already on your way. You may already know that you work best at night or in the mornings.

If you don't, it's easy to discover your natural rhythms. You can do this by monitoring your feelings and energy level throughout the day. This is a simple experiment and the results may surprise you. You may discover things you never knew about your energy patterns.

Get a notebook or a day planner. Decide on a regular time throughout the day to "check in." You should have at least one check-in for each part of the day (morning, noon, afternoon, evening, night, etc.) but the more often you check-in the better.

For each check-in, jot down a quick note on how you're feeling or how your work is going. You could create a system such as a number from one to five. Five means you're blazing right along and getting things done; one means you'd be better off taking a nap. By making your check-ins quick and easy, you can check-in more often during the day, which makes your results more accurate.

Rhythmless Nation

Establishing Routines

Now I know I just told you to SWIIIIITCH it up, however we all know that you must have a routine as well. Good routines help you formulate good habits.

Whichever process you choose, take the data and create a schedule from it. Create a routine for each part of the day. In doing this, you create an expected behavior and this makes it easier to stay focused. But remember, if you are getting bored or losing your focus, SWIIIIITCH!!!

It can be difficult to plan every single task that you perform each day. For this reason, it may be useful to create task categories. These are categories such as:

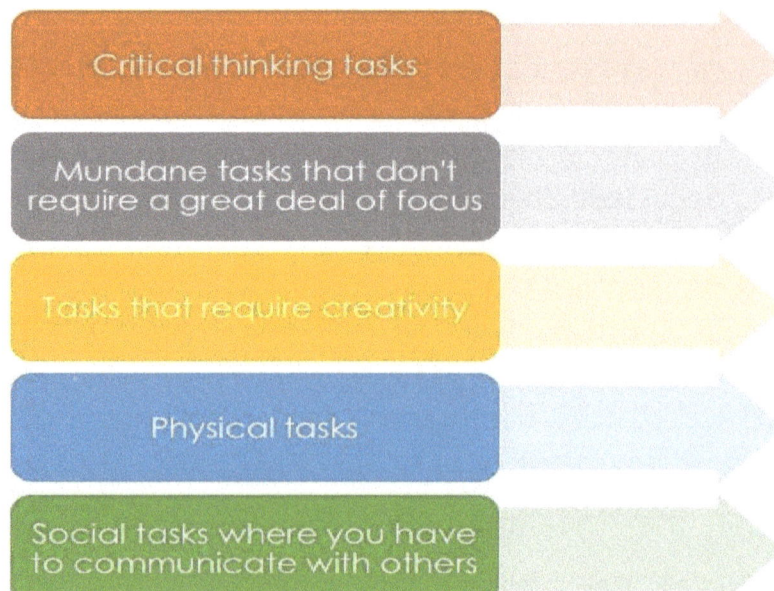

Critical thinking tasks

Mundane tasks that don't require a great deal of focus

Tasks that require creativity

Physical tasks

Social tasks where you have to communicate with others

Rythmless Nation

You can plug each task into one of the above categories. For example, social media, email and meetings might go into the social category. Trying to come up with product ideas or writing content would be creative tasks. Critical thinking tasks include a great deal of problem solving. Well you get the drift.

You can decide on a schedule that looks something like this:

Early Morning: Critical thinking tasks
Late Morning: Communications
Afternoon: Routine tasks
Evening: Creative tasks

An easier method is to simply identify the focus level you need for each task. You can create your own rating system or just identify those that require a great deal of focus. You can then identify your level of focus for each part of the day and then schedule your tasks accordingly.

Rhythmless Nation

Identify your energy levels at different times of day. Note what work you prefer to do at those times of day.

Energy Levels	Preferred Work To Do
e.g., 9am-11am – High energy	Social Media Updates
	Check Email

Rhythmless Nation

Based on your high-energy and low energy times, outline a morning, mid-day, and evening routine to follow.

Time of Day	Work To Do
EARLY MORNING	
LATE MORNING	
AFTERNOON	
EVENING	

Manage Your "Time Drains"

Manage Your "Time Drains"

So far, we've talked about how to harness your focus for the best productivity possible. As we said in the introduction, the other way you improve your productivity is by removing things that block it. In this chapter we'll talk about "time drains" – things that eat away at your time and keep you from getting things done.

Keep in mind that time drains aren't necessarily time wasters. But they're things you need to control and keep in check. They won't harm your productivity if you can effectively manage them. If you don't, you will be headed for a downward spiral.

Manage Your "Time Drains"

You've Got Mail

We mentioned turning off notifications when we discussed focus, but for many of us that's not enough. You may also be a compulsive email checker, quickly checking your inbox throughout the day. Email is important and you need to know if someone is trying to get in touch with you, but it can also be a time drain.

There are several ways you can better manage your email and reduce the time you spend on it. One is to establish a time during the day for handling emails. Some emails only need a quick reply from you, but others are more involved. Create a scheduled time for reading and responding to these important emails.

For emails that may get long and involved, send the person a quick message telling them that you've received the message and you'll send a detailed reply later. If there's a particularly urgent email, add responding to it to your to-do list. Decide on its priority level and add it to your things to do.

Manage Your "Time Drains"

Another method for controlling email time is to set a time limit, similar to what you did with the kitchen timer. Check your email for twenty minutes in the morning and twenty minutes in the afternoon. When looking at your inbox, quickly choose the message that's most urgent or important. You only have twenty minutes, so you need to prioritize and make decisions quickly.

You can also save time by better organizing your email inbox. Create a folder labeled "important" for high priority items, and check this folder first each time. Separate your work and personal email accounts so that personal emails don't distract you. Create an 'away' message telling the sender that you'll get back to them as soon as possible. You can also create email templates and 'canned responses' for similar emails or email responses you commonly send.

Manage Your "Time Drains"

www

It often happens that you get online for a specific piece of information and before you know it, you're looking at funny cat memes. The Internet offers a wealth of distractions to keep you from getting things done. When you get on the Internet, keep one goal in mind (that specific bit of information or the one task you need to accomplish) . Avoid looking at sidebars and close the browser after finding the information or completing the task. If there's something else you want to see, bookmark it and go back to it later.

Social media is a particularly dangerous time drain. Try logging out of your social media accounts and only log in when you're ready to focus on it for a specific length of time. Turn off notifications from social media apps on your phone, and use any downtime, such as waiting in line at a store, to respond to messages via your mobile device. If social media is part of what you need to do each day, add social media time to your daily schedule and stay on task when using it.

Manage Your "Time Drains"

Can You Hear Me Now?

"Hello from the other siiiide!" You know you have to sing that right? Don't you just love Adele's song! LOL!

Do you remember when there were no cell phones and you only had one line with noooooo voice mail? I do. And we survived. I get that calls are important but not every call is. To minimize the negative effect a call can have on your productivity, keep calls focused on important business. If it's not urgent, schedule a time to call the person back later in the day when you have a little more time to chat it up, like while you are sitting in traffic, or let it go to a voice mail message that tells people when they can expect a reply. If you can't control the urge to answer every call that you receive, again, turn the phone off or give it to someone else to filter urgent calls for you during certain times. YOU ARE IN CONTROL OF YOUR TIME!

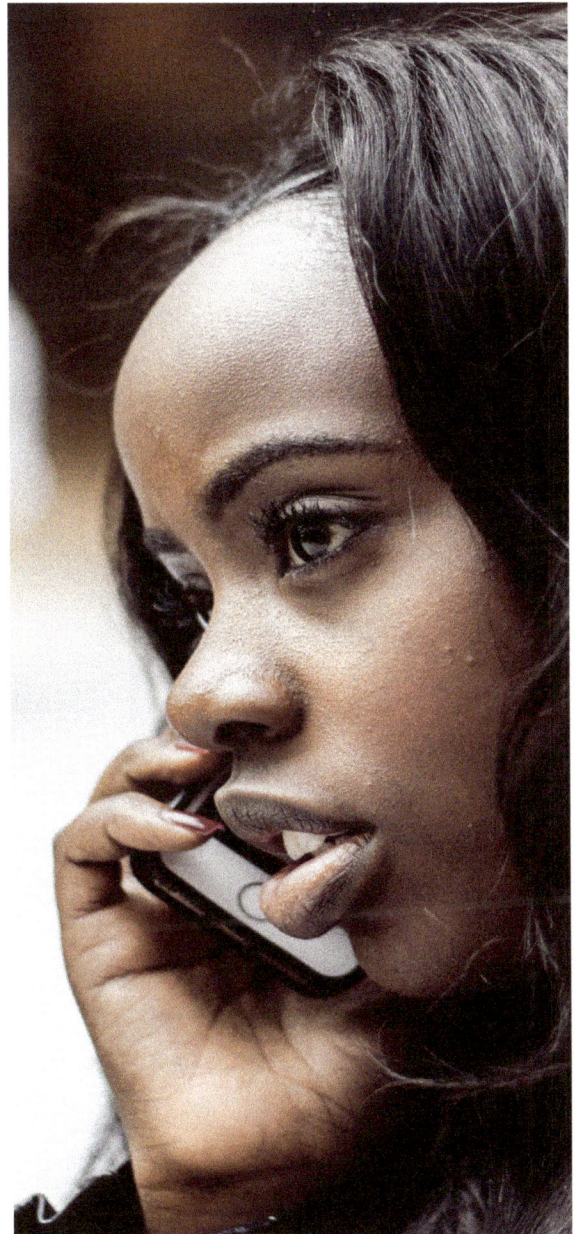

Manage Your "Time Drains"

It's Just Business

You may be struggling with time management at work. Between meetings and your "cubicle cousins", I mean co-workers, you can't seem to get anything done.

Organize meetings so that they are as short as possible and have a clear starting and ending time. Create a detailed agenda and timing for the meetings so that they stay focused on important business. And make sure people know what they need to do before attending the meeting. Assign someone to keep you on track with time especially if you are a talker like me.

Technology is great now and you can meet online. Try doing this as much as possible. It will definitely save you time especially if you have to travel to the meeting. Skype, Google Hangouts, Zoom and Webex are just a few tools you can use for online meetings.

Manage Your "Time Drains"

There are several ways to handle those "cubicle cousins" of yours if they present a distraction. One is not being afraid to say no to requests or to tell people that you're busy. Either offer your coworkers a time when you could handle the situation or refer them to someone else who might be available. You don't want to seem like you're shutting them out. Offer whatever help you can to get their problem solved.

You may want to schedule times to chat, socialize and blow off steam with your coworkers. This could be a nice break to help you keep your focus during working time.

Manage Your "Time Drains"

The Same Ole Same Ole

Many tasks are a time drain, even though they need to be done. These are tasks that are routine and mundane, and that anyone can do. Although essential, these tasks take away from more important tasks such as problem solving, creative work or critical thinking. They may take away from tasks that require your special skills; in other words, tasks only you can do.

There are four ways to get rid of these mundane tasks:

1. **ELIMINATE**
   Ask yourself whether the task really needs to be done. Does it actually deliver any tangible result or is it just something you do out of habit? If it's the latter, cross it off your to-do list permanently.

2. **DELEGATE**
   Find someone else in your circle who can do the work for you. Find someone who is less busy or who has fewer specialized tasks and reassign the work to them.

Manage Your "Time Drains"

3. **OUTSOURCE**

   Find help outside of your circle for routine tasks. You can outsource many types of online tasks to a virtual assistant.

4. **AUTOMATE**

   Look for online tools, software programs and organizational tools that can help you handle repetitive work.

Mindless Entertainment

A great number of our time drains are simply mindless entertainment (Housewives of Atlanta, Married to Medicine, Black Ink, Love & ......Oh my bad. I drifted.) LOL! Especially if you're working at home, you may find video games, TV, music, social media, YouTube videos, kids, online solitaire and virtually anything else fun and entertaining eating away at your time.

We need these distractions. They give us pleasure and take our minds off of the work we have to do. It's okay to spend some of your time indulging in these leisure activities, but you just need to be in control of it. However if you always "chase the rabbit", cut it out completely until you can become self-disciplined.

To help you be able to control this, set your trusty timer and when your time is up...IT'S UP! Resume your tasks and get back on track. Another idea is to set aside a certain time of day to indulge to your heart's content. Naturally, the end of the day is perfect for this. After lunch is another good time to take an extended fun break.

Manage Your "Time Drains" ACTIVITY

1. Review your answers to all the activities you've completed so far. Can you identify any patterns that show where your biggest time drains are?

2. If not, try tracking exactly what you spend your time on each day for a week and add up the time for each task. You can use a simple notepad, or a tool like Evernote.

3. Once you've done the above, make a list of which items are taking up too much of your time relative to their importance for achieving your goals.

1	
2	
3	
4	
5	
6	
7	
8	
9	
10	

Manage Your "Time Drains" ACTIVITY

IT'S TIME TO PUT IN THE WORK!!!

4. Now on the next page, note which tips from this chapter you're going to implement to eliminate or reduce these time drains.

Manage Your "Time Drains"
ACTIVITY

TIPS	CHECK
EMAILS	
Establish time for handling emails	
Send a short reply and note to respond later to long emails	
Set a time limit for writing emails	
Organize your email inbox with separate folders	
THE INTERNET	
Keep your goal in mind when online	
Close your browser when you're done	
Log out of Social Media accounts	
Turn off notifications	
Add Social Media time to your schedule	
PHONE CALLS	
Keep calls focused on business	
Schedule call backs	
Delegate phones to others	
MEETINGS	
Keep meetings to a minimum	
Only discuss issues that aren't easily discussed via email	
Organize with a clear start and ending time	
Make sure people know what the need to do before attending	
Use online meetings to avoid travel time	
Agree on a regular meeting time	
COWORKERS	
Create a physically isolated environment	
Know how to say no to requests	
Schedule times to chat and blow off steam	
MUNDANE TASKS	
Eliminate – Does it really need to be done?	
Delegate – Find someone in your organization who is less busy to do the work	
Outsource – Find help outside of your organization	
Automate – Look for online tools and programs to help	
MINDLESS ENTERTAINMENT	
Spend a little time indulging but maintain control	
Do fun activities during your break times	
Make sure you can easily pull yourself away	
Set a timer	
Set aside time each day to indulge	

Organized Mess....NOT!!!

Organized Mess....NOT!!!

Clutter:To fill or litter with things in a disorderly manner; state or condition of confusion.

No matter how affectionate you may feel toward your beloved clutter, when you are organized, you will live a more productive life. I know you are saying, "But I have organized clutter!" Yeeeaaah....NO. That is no longer going to work. When everything around you is cluttered, it's actually a reflection of your mind and this is why those that are organized find it easier to focus and get things done when they have an organized system in place.

Organized Mess....NOT!!!

Organizing your life can be challenging because of the amount of stuff (clutter) you have physically and mentally. Most people think of papers, clothes or just stuff when you say clutter. But you can be in a mental state of clutter too. Think about it. If you are wanting to start a business, it's hard to concentrate on the things of the business when you look around your house and laundry needs to be done, the kitchen needs to be cleaned, mail needs to be put way, etc. Your mind is cluttered with the things needing to be done. So to help with managing your time, you must declutter. Let's review a few steps to help you declutter physically.

Keep Surfaces Clean

Put It Away

Go Paperless

A Zone For Important Stuff

A Zone For Current Stuff

Identify Trouble Spots

Consider Off-site Storage

Start From Scratch

Organized Mess....NOT!!!

Keep Surfaces Clean

The main trouble area for clutter is surfaces. Your desktop, shelves, kitchen counters, filing cabinet tops, and so on, are where clutter is most likely to accumulate. You can create whatever kind of filing system you want, but at the very least make sure that your surfaces stay clean.

Put It Away

As soon as you use something, put it away immediately. I know I have struggled with this especially when it came to putting away clothes. I have a couch in my bedroom and all of the worn clothes seemed to have ended up there until I simply said "this is ridiculous." LOL! So I started getting undressed in my closet so I could put things where they belong. I found that taking two minutes to do that saved me hours on a Saturday. So after using anything, PUT IT AWAY! Get into a habit of doing this and it'll be second nature.

Organized Mess....NOT!!!

Go Paperless

A great deal of clutter comes from papers. If you are like me, you have a certain area or bin that mail goes in however it just seems to pile up. But in today's world of technology, automation and paperless options, there's little need for all the paper you may collect. Whenever possible, go paperless. Scan documents and store files digitally. Going paperless not only reduces the clutter paperwork causes but is also good for the environment.

A Zone For Important Stuff

Create one particular space for important things that need to be dealt with as soon as possible. This is one part of your workspace where it's okay to pile things up. Make it something like your inbox and set aside at least a little time each day for going through these important things to-do.

A Zone For Current Stuff

You might also want to create a space for files and things related to any current or ongoing projects. For current projects, you may need to access these files often and it's a drain on your time to keep filing and retrieving them. When the project is done, file this stuff with your regular files.

Organized Mess....NOT!!!

Identify Troubled Spots

In every workspace, there are certain areas where things tend to pile up. This could be an area that's used by many people or an area that's simply a convenient place to put things. Identify this spot and pay especially close attention to it, making sure that things don't pile up there. If necessary, create a special tidying plan for handling this area.

Consider Off-Site Storage

If lack of storage space causes clutter, consider off-site storage. There may be a lot of things that you have around that can simply be stored off-site such as different holiday decorations, papers that you are just keeping for tax purposes or furniture that's really not being used and is simply in the way. There are so many storage facilities popping up, the monthly cost is nominal and will be worth it in the end.

Organized Mess....NOT!!!

Start From Scratch

You know how when you clean your house, it seems to get messier before it gets clean especially if you are purging? Well getting organized is just like that. Sometimes you just have to START OVER!!

If there is a space you need to declutter, remove everything and start from scratch. Take everything out of that area and only bring back what you need. If there are items you never feel the need to replace, you didn't need them. But here's the thing. Don't keep those items. Either discard them or put them in storage. Remember your goal is to create organization so your time can be managed and you can become the best YOU!

Organized Mess....NOT!!!

Look around your space and make notes on what you need to do to de-clutter, along with any supplies you need. Set aside a block of time to do the initial tidying up. Then set aside another time at the end of each day to clear it up.

What Needs To Be Done

_____
_____
_____
_____
_____
_____
_____
_____
_____
_____
_____
_____
_____
_____
_____
_____
_____
_____
_____
_____
_____
_____
_____
_____
_____

Be Selective

Be Selective

To bolster your productivity, you need to be highly selective about what tasks you decide to do yourself. We've covered choosing and prioritizing tasks already, but here are some tips to help you become more selective about which tasks you do.

The 80/20 Rule

In terms of results, not all tasks are equal. The 80/20 Rule is a well-known concept used in sales. It says that 80% of your revenue comes from 20% of your customers. Salespeople, in order to maximize their efforts, must identify and focus on those 20%. For your productivity, the 80/20 Rules says that 20% of your efforts lead to 80% of your results. Being selective means identifying those tasks that lead to the greater results.

Review Your Goals

Start by reviewing your goals. Make sure that every task on your list of things to do is in accordance with your goals. If a task isn't, move it down your list of priorities or move it to your alternative list. The things you put the highest priority on should be goal-oriented.

Keep in mind that we're not just talking about short-term goals here. Long-term goals should also be given high priority. Goals such as growing your business are things that you may not have daily tasks for, but this doesn't mean they aren't important. These long-term goals can get lost in the shuffle when there are many daily tasks to attend to.

Be Selective

Prioritize By Results

Earlier we discussed prioritizing your list according to set deadlines. Another way to be selective is to organize by the results each task produces. For example, one task may produce immediate earnings for you while another works toward a more distant goal. Today, your concern may be maximizing earnings, so you would give the former a higher priority.

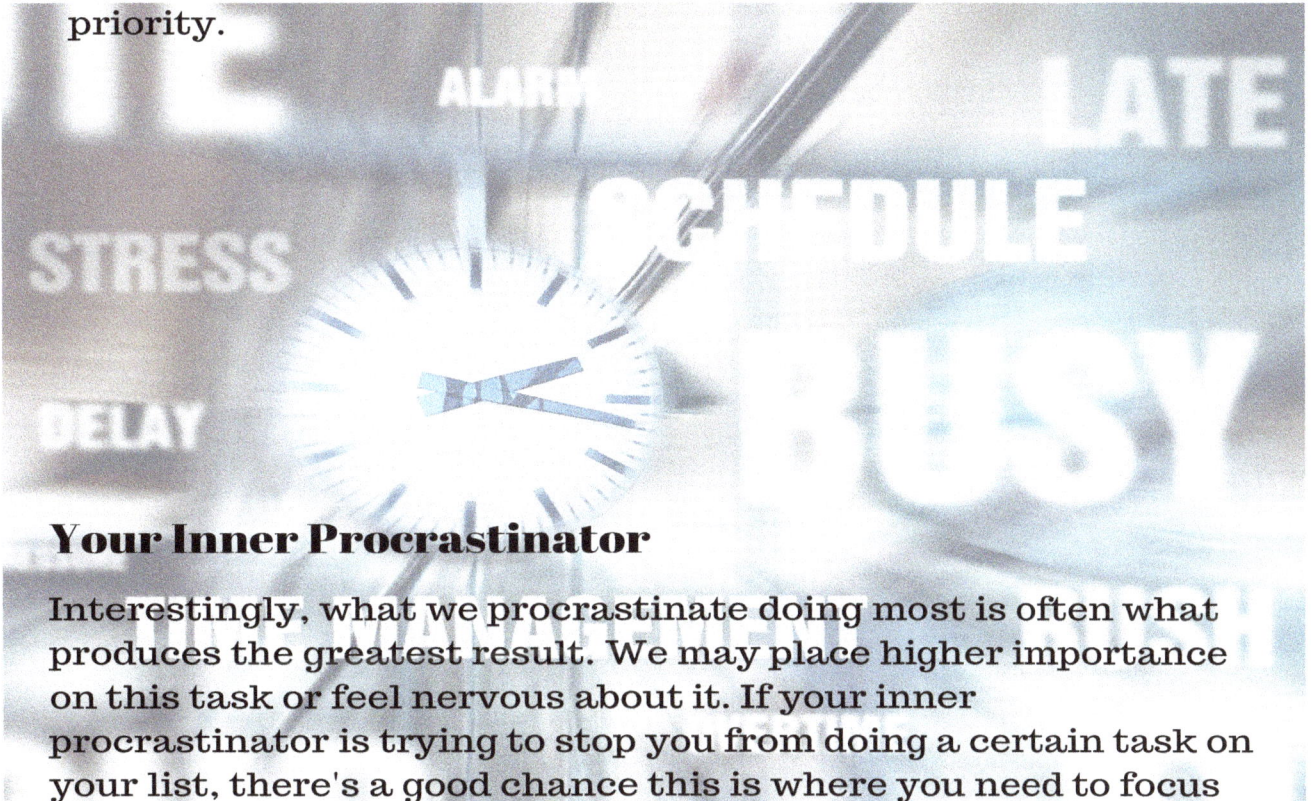

Your Inner Procrastinator

Interestingly, what we procrastinate doing most is often what produces the greatest result. We may place higher importance on this task or feel nervous about it. If your inner procrastinator is trying to stop you from doing a certain task on your list, there's a good chance this is where you need to focus your efforts. In the words of Nike...JUST DO IT!

Be Selective

Be Secure In Your NO

If you deal with requests from other people on a daily basis, learn to say no and be secure in it. You want to be a helpful person and a good team player, but there's a time to say yes and a time to say no. We discussed ideas for doing this in the previous chapter on time drains, so choose which are the most appropriate for you. Most importantly, don't feel like you have to drop everything the instant someone needs help. Develop the habit of turning down requests for now so that you don't clutter your daily schedule.

Set Expectations

Set expectations for others in terms of things like availability and reply time. In general, don't reply to emails immediately. This sets a precedent that you're not always available. You may also want to tell others the specific times when you're available to communicate. Business associates contacting you don't want to wait, but if they know that they can reach you easily at a certain time, it won't affect your reliability.

Be Selective

Opportunities

You don't want something to come along and distract you, but you also don't want to miss a good opportunity. The best way to deal with this is to take a minute to consider the opportunity and the effect it will have on your productivity in other areas. Make a plan for the time you'll lose on everything else or add extra time to your schedule to deal with the new opportunity. If these opportunities come along often, you can create a schedule where you allow extra time that's unassigned to any particular task. You have to be strict yet fluid with your schedule. I know that sounds crazy but it's true. There's no such thing as balance but you can strive for harmony.

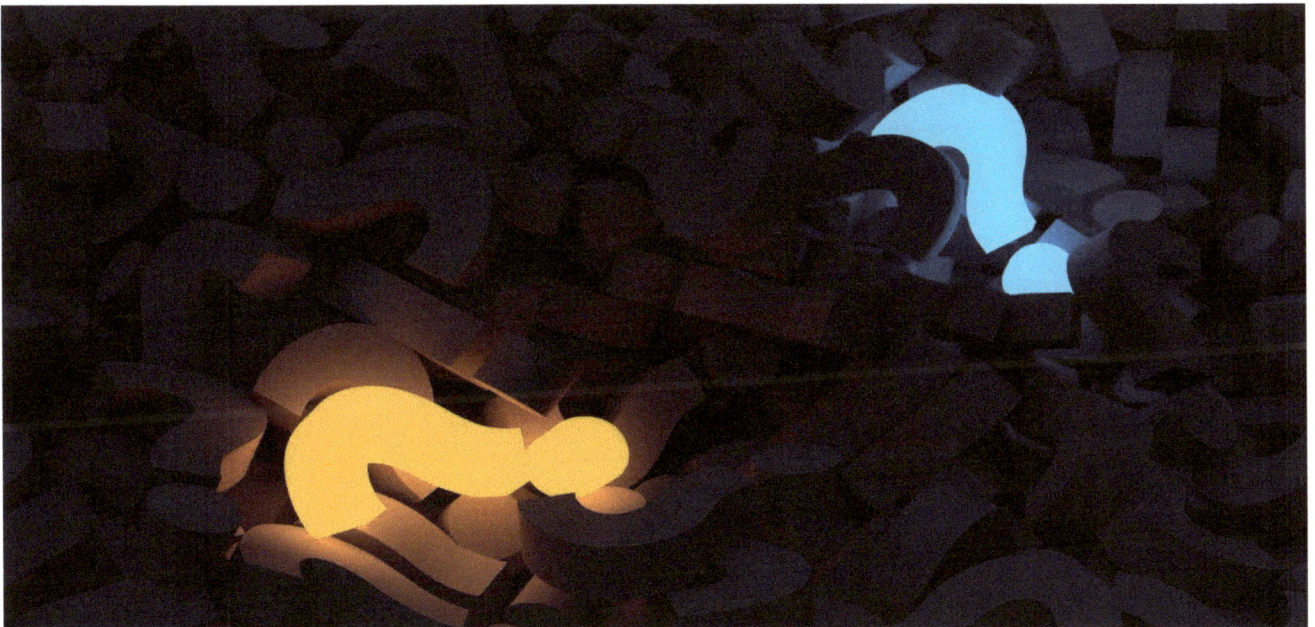

Be Selective

Make a list of your top goals for your business. Then highlight the top 3. Refer to this whenever you create a to-do list.

1	
2	
3	
4	
5	
6	
7	
8	
9	
10	

Now, review your current to-do list. Which items are essential to achieving your goals? Which items could be eliminated without affecting your business?
Refine your list by removing all items that are not related to achieving your top 3 goals.

Your Health Is Your Wealth

Your Health Is Your Wealth

Your body and mind need to be in good health in order to be as productive as you can be. There are whole books and courses dedicated to each aspect of personal healthcare, but in this chapter, we're going to tackle the major issues and offer simple solutions.

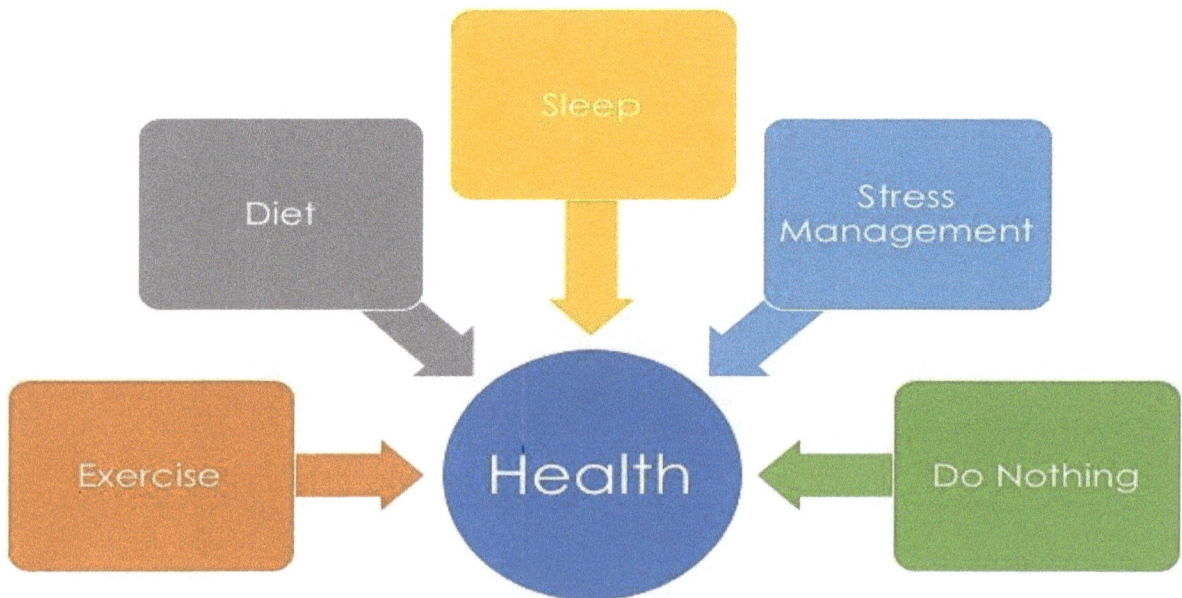

Sleep

Diet

Stress Management

Exercise

Health

Do Nothing

Your Health Is Your Wealth

Get Moving

You should be getting at least moderate exercise on a regular basis. This means getting out and doing something physical two to three times a week. This is especially important if you spend all day in front of the computer and even more critical if your hobbies don't involve physical activity.

When the blood is pumping through your body, this has an effect on your mind. People who start exercising after years of no exercise always report elevated energy levels and better focus. Exercise also helps you blow off steam, reduce stress, and mitigate the health risks associated with spending all day at a desk.

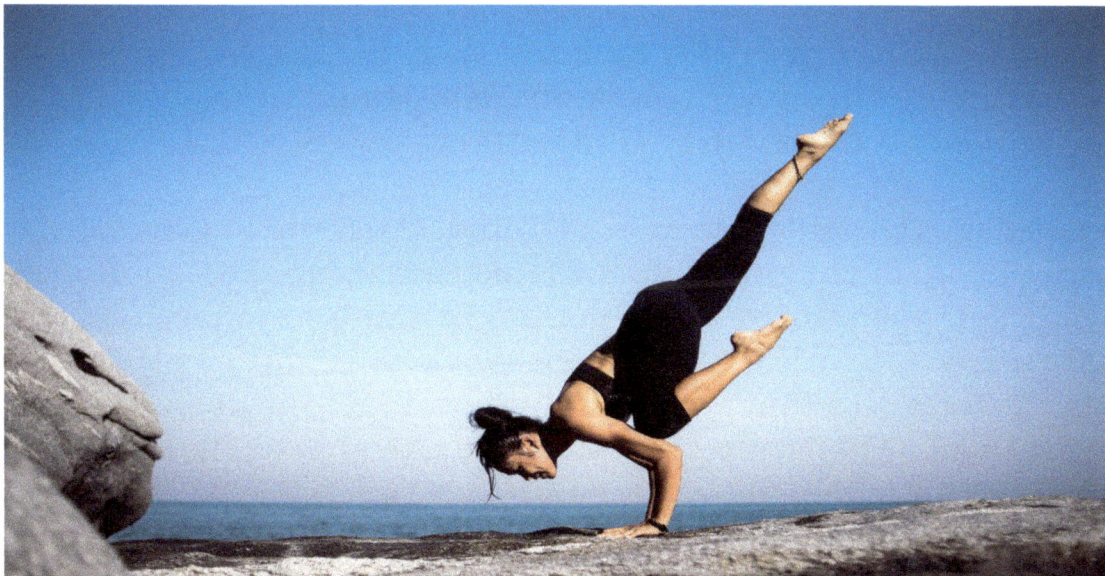

Your Health Is Your Wealth

Eat Right

Eat three balanced meals a day and have a snack time if necessary. If your stomach is empty, you'll lose focus because your brain isn't getting the nutrients it needs. Don't rush meals. Take your time and enjoy them. Don't skip breakfast for the sake of productivity. The first meal of the day is as important as everyone says it is.

Snack breaks are great for keeping your focus throughout the day, but make sure your snack choices are healthy. Sugary and fatty foods can have the reverse effect.

Another diet consideration is caffeine. Caffeine is great for getting us up in the morning and keeping us sharp – in moderate amounts. If one cup of coffee makes you more focused, three must turn you into a productivity machine, right? The answer to this is a resounding no. Too much caffeine makes you jittery and unable to concentrate. If you like caffeinated drinks, watch your intake.

Your Health Is Your Wealth

You Must Rest

The image of the Highly Productive Individual is one who sleeps three hours a day so they can spend as much time as possible pumping out work. Unfortunately, this is a largely mythical figure. Most of us can't function deprived of sleep. Lack of sleep or bad sleeping habits can lead to trouble focusing and lost productivity.

Sleeping schedules and habits differ from person to person, but you should be getting enough sleep, regular sleep and good sleep. If you're constantly feeling lethargic, sleep habits are a likely cause. If you sleep long hours but wake up not feeling rested, this is an indication that you may have a sleep disorder keeping you from getting the deep sleep you need.

Some people find that a shorter sleep at night with naps during the day helps with their productivity. Some people swear by the "power nap," where you lie down for 10 minutes of intense napping. Try the power nap and see if it helps you recharge.

Your Health Is Your Wealth

Stress Free

Make sure you're dealing with stress in a healthy way. If you make sure that you're exercising, eating well and sleeping enough, this will help. But it's also good to have a few stress reduction techniques on hand to help you relax. These techniques could be exercises like meditation, yoga or light exercise; they could be hobbies like reading or listening to music; or they could be more in-depth practices like creative visualization and deep breathing.

Have a few long-term and a few short-term stress reduction techniques on hand. Long-term techniques are things you practice regularly over time to reduce your overall stress level; for example, you might meditate for twenty minutes at the start of each day.

A short-term technique is something you do when something sets you off and you need to calm down and regain your focus. For example, your computer crashes and it sends you off into a spiral of rage. This is a good time to go for a quick run or spend a little quality time with your favorite video game.

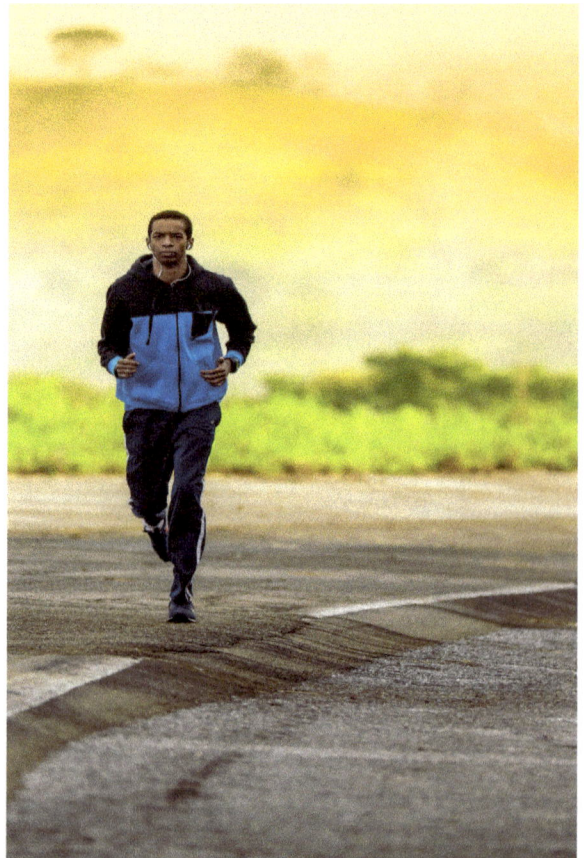

Your Health Is Your Wealth

Be Still

Somewhere in your busy schedule, you need some time to simply sit and do nothing at all. With all of our gadgets and modern entertainment, moments of silence have become rare. Even when taking a break or performing daily routines like brushing your teeth, you're scrolling through your Twitter feed or listening to the TV news in the other room.

But this silent time is important for your mental health. You should spend at least a little time each day doing absolutely nothing. Just sit on the couch and let your mind wander for a few minutes. It can help you reduce the feeling of clutter in your brain, which then allows you to focus better when you're working.

Your Health Is Your Wealth

Review the tips from the chapter and identify where your own health is reducing your productivity.

Tips	Your Own Health
Exercise	
Diet	
Sleep	
Stress Management	
Do Nothing	

Your Health Is Your Wealth

Note which tips you'll implement right away and how you'll do it.

Tips	How You'll Implement
Exercise	
Diet	
Sleep	
Stress Management	
Do Nothing	

Conclusion

Conclusion

Time management is a dedicated process but you must also be fluid. I hope I have done a pretty good job of covering the main aspects. Think of this E-book as a toolbox full of ideas. By selecting a variety of techniques, you can immediately start making changes and managing your time more efficiently and effectively. You'll accomplish tasks faster and better, and as a result, you'll have plenty of time to spend on other things.

Productivity isn't something you learn once and then forget about. You should always be monitoring your work to see where things can be tightened up. Keep looking for areas where you can delegate, automate or outsource. Keep your eyes out for new tools that can help you improve your productivity.

Productivity isn't a skill, it's a mindset. Change your mindset and... **BECOME THE BEST YOU!!!**

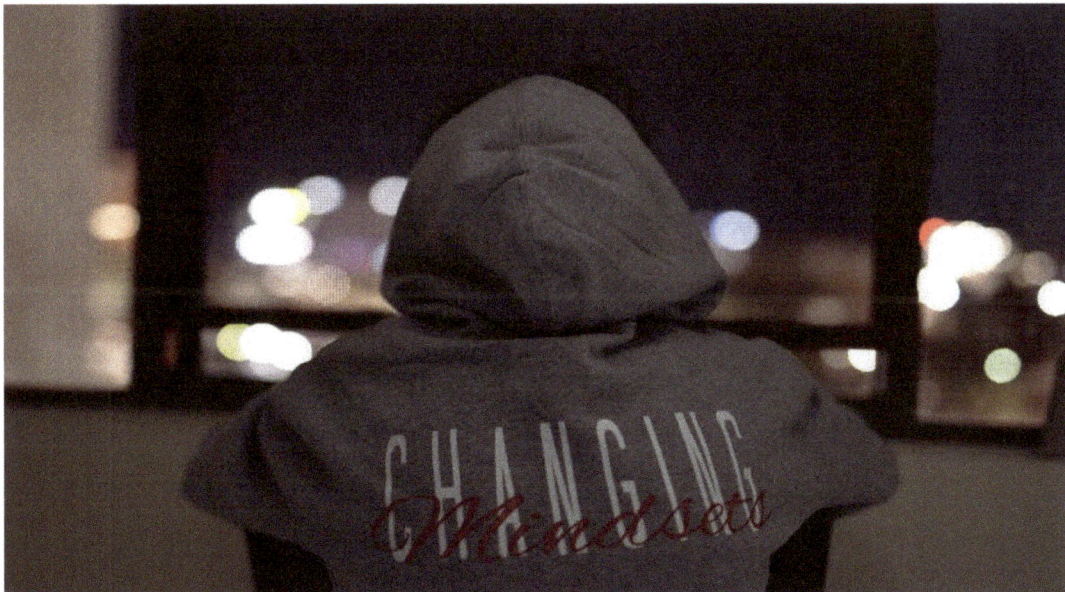

3G Publishing, Inc.
Loganville, Ga 30052
www.3gpublishinginc.com
Phone: 1-888-442-9637

©2020, Mary Boyde. All rights reserved.

No part of this book may be reproduced, stored in a retrieval system,
or transmitted by any means without the written permission of the author.

First published by 3G Publishing, Inc. December 2020

ISBN: 9781941247846

Printed in the United States of America

Because of the dynamic nature of the Internet, any web addresses or links contained in this book
may have changed since publication and may no longer be valid. The views expressed in this
work are solely those of the author and do not necessarily reflect the views of the publisher, and
the publisher hereby disclaims any responsibility for them.